# information security

best practice measures for
protecting your business

consultant editor:         Marc Beishon
sub-editor:                Lesley Malachowski
production manager:        Lisa Robertson
design:                    Halo Design
commercial director:       Ed Hicks
publishing director:       Tom Nash
chief operating officer:   Andrew Main Wilson
chairman:                  Miles Templeman

Published for the Institute of Directors
and the DTI by Director Publications Ltd
116 Pall Mall London SW1Y 5ED
☏ 020 7766 8950  🖳 www.iod.com

© Copyright May 2005 Director Publications Ltd
A CIP record for this book is available from the British Library
Printed and bound in Great Britain.

# CONTENTS

# DTI 'HOW TO' GUIDES & CHECK LISTS

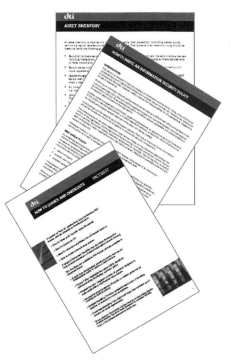

The DTI publishes a number of 'How To' Guides and Check Lists to help organisations apply best practice to protect their business information.

The following 'How To' guides have been produced in PDF and are available to download (see web site address below) 'How To':

- Write an IT Security Policy Document
- Choose an ISP
- Outsource and Make Use of External Services
- Protect yourself from viruses

A range of Document Checklists has also been developed to help promote awareness of critical information security issues. The following checklists are available in PDF and are also available to download from the DTI web site:

- E-mail.
- Privacy Policy.
- Physical Security.
- Information Asset Inventory.
- Incident Handling.
- Good Housekeeping.

Information Security Policy Team
Department of Trade and Industry
151 Buckingham Palace Road
London SW1W 9SS
Tel:      020 7215 1962
Fax:      020 7215 1966
email:    infosecpolicyteam@dti.gsi.gov.uk
Web:      www.dti.gov.uk/industries/information_security

# getting the basics right

**Miles Templeman, Director General
Institute of Directors**

The Information and Communication Technology (ICT) tools developed over the last decade are having a major impact on enterprises of all sizes. Across the globe, we are now generating and storing two exabytes (two billion gigabytes) of information each year.

Enterprises in the developed world are increasingly learning how to exploit this information that their businesses create, as we move to a more 'knowledge-driven' economy. The careful deployment of new ICT, within the context of managed business change, has added one per cent per year to USA GDP over at least the last ten years. The UK is not far behind the USA and significantly ahead of many of our European competitors.

However, there is a bewildering array of new ICT developments such as intranets, extranets, data warehouses and business intelligence systems, all clustered around affordable 'always on' broadband access to the global Internet. As with any set of new processes and tools, these ICT developments offer new vulnerabilities and pitfalls as well as clear top and bottom line benefits. It is imperative that they are treated with care and respect. As a senior police officer once said: "there are no new crimes, just new ways of committing old crimes." The new ICT tools offer all sorts of new ways of subverting old business processes often simply through the action of disaffected or dishonest employees.

This Director's Guide explains the context of ICT security, both fixed and on the move, and provides clear and straightforward guidance on directors' responsibilities and how to get the basics right.

# The New ISO/IEC 17799 Standard

In June/July this year the international business community will see the publication of the new version of ISO/IEC 17799.

The first edition of the Code of Practice BS 7799 (Part 1) was published in 1995. Over the last decade this standard has been revised, road tested and developed into the international standard ISO/IEC 17799. The first edition of ISO/IEC 17799 was published in 2000 and now in 2005 a new version will be available.

This best practice standard is now a universal 'common language' for information security management for businesses around the world.

## ISO/IEC 17799 Revision Highlights

*Aims have been to*
- *Keep the 2000 edition of Best Practice up to date and include new developments, new threats, and evolving requirements*
- *Maintain backwards compatibility with the 2000 edition*
- *Improve and clarify Best Practice in the international context*

*Drivers*
- *Address due diligence and governance and regulatory compliance*
- *Provide customer assurance*
- *Address outsourcing and external service arrangements*
- *Manage risks*
- *Assess/demonstrate being 'fit for purpose'*

*Some Areas of Change (additional controls, improvements and updates to existing controls)*
- *Asset Management (including asset ownership and acceptable use of assets and resources)*
- *Human Resources (to include before, during and termination of employment security issues)*
- *Malicious Code (to include mobile code)*
- *External Access( business partners, service providers, outsourcing arrangement, customers)*
- *Service delivery management*
- *Information security incident management*
- *Management of patches and other vulnerabilities*

## Further Information

Copies of the new standard will be available from:  BSI Publications - orders@bsi-global.com
For details of the other ISMS standards, certification to BS 7799 Part 2 and the International Certification Register go to the ISMS International User Group web site www.xisec.com
For other information security enquires contact the DTI Team on infosecpolicyteam@dti.gsi.gov.uk

# building trust in technology

**David Hendon, Director,
Business Relations, DTI**

We tend to forget how recently the Internet has entered our lives and it is difficult now to think how we would manage without it supporting both our business and private lives. Looking back, it is now hard to believe the extent to which the Internet was born in a spirit of idealism bordering on innocence. Indeed, the first occurrences of what we now call Denial of Service attacks were aimed at individuals accused of using the Internet for commercial purposes.

It is now generally accepted that one of the major challenges facing the developed economies is the extent to which they can establish a competitive position in how they use the new technologies to transform their economies. The DTI has understood this fact for many years and it is a major feature of our engagement with business across the board.

At the same time, we have also always accepted that establishing business confidence in the new technologies is an essential requirement if we are to stay at the forefront of economies in the information age. I am glad to count the IoD as one of our key partners in that effort and I am sure a wide range of business readers will find this publication both stimulating and a practical tool in achieving secure information management in their businesses. I am grateful to the IoD for inviting the DTI to partner them in this enterprise.

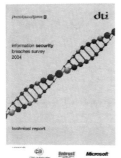

# DTI Information Security Breaches Survey

DTI Breaches Survey 2004

Legend:
- ISBS 2004 - large businesses
- ISBS 2004 - overall
- ISBS 2002 - overall

Chart: DTI Breaches Survey 2004

| Category | ISBS 2004 - large businesses | ISBS 2004 - overall | ISBS 2002 - overall |
|---|---|---|---|
| Virus infection and disruptive software | 68% | 50% | 41% |
| Staff misuse of information systems | 64% | 22% | 11% |
| Unauthorised access by outsiders (including hacking attempts) | 38% | 17% | 14% |
| Theft or fraud involving computers | 49% | 11% | 6% |
| Systems failure or data corruption* | 42% | 27% | N/A* |

(axis: 0  10  20  30  40  50  60  70)

Since 1991, the Department of Trade and Industry has sponsored research into information security breaches to help UK businesses better understand the risks they face. The Information Security Breaches Survey 2004 (ISBS 2004) is the seventh such survey.

The information security breaches survey has over the last decade formed an integral part of the DTI's programme to help UK businesses address the issue of information security. The survey results show that the UK is now firmly in the Information Age, with companies of all sizes embracing the use of the Internet. This is changing the way that business operates, improving efficiency and customer service. However, a side effect of this increased connectivity is greater exposure to information security issues. Indeed, this survey shows that security problems have now become a fact of business life, and not something that happens to someone else. As organisations struggle to contain these threats, the number of security incidents continues to rise.

To order or download the 2004 survey, please visit the DTI site www.dti.gov.uk/industries/information_security

Information Security Policy Team
Department of Trade and Industry
151 Buckingham Palace Road
London SW1W 9SS
Tel:       020 7215 1962
Fax:       020 7215 1966
email:    infosecpolicyteam@dti.gsi.gov.uk

# security is a boardroom issue

Information security management plays a key role in supporting a company's governance, risk management and compliance efforts, says Chris Potter, partner, PricewaterhouseCoopers LLP, and co-author of the 2002 and 2004 DTI Information Security Breaches Surveys

The curse of gamblers, politicians and science fiction writers is that predicting the future is difficult. In some respects, the world changes very quickly. In others, it stays the same.

## beam me up, Scotty

Take the example of Star Trek, the television show. Piloted in 1966 and set in 2262, its characters carried mobile phone communicators and transferred data on small disk-like objects. Both of these seem mundane to us now. And the Starship Enterprise's computer room is positively antediluvian, with tape drives the size of wardrobes. Our use of technology has advanced faster in these areas than anyone would have guessed in the 1960s.

### EXECUTIVE SUMMARY

- [ ] information security has never been more important than now
- [ ] it's a worldwide phenomenon, driven by changes in the way businesses use technology
- [ ] it fits into the board's overall view of governance, risk management and compliance
- [ ] there's a gap between apparent priority and actual activity in many businesses

On the other hand, Star Trek's interstellar travel, teleportation and moneyless society still retain their futuristic flavour. Space travel, in particular, has advanced less quickly than we imagined in the heady days of the Space Race. In the

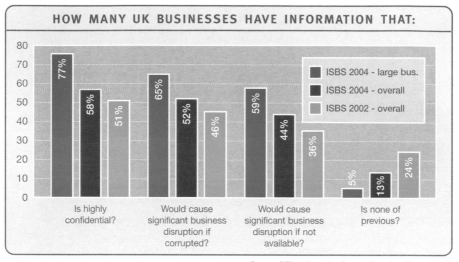

HOW MANY UK BUSINESSES HAVE INFORMATION THAT:

Source: DTI's Information Security Breaches Survey (ISBS)

same way, while the business world we inhabit today is in some senses very similar to that a decade ago, in others it is a radically different environment.

The biggest of these changes is the Internet. According to the DTI's Information Security Breaches Survey 2004, nine-tenths of UK businesses with a computer now send email across the Internet, browse the web and have a website. Most websites now allow customers to initiate transactions online. Small and medium-sized businesses tend to use a simple externally hosted online store, or just allow customers to email them orders. Websites of larger businesses tend to be a fully integrated channel into core business systems.

But, it's not just the Internet. Network boundaries are extending as businesses increasingly allow their staff to access systems remotely. Over half of UK businesses now do this. Personal digital assistants (PDAs) are also being used to provide easy access to business information on the move. A third of businesses (and half of large ones) now use these devices. Finally, adoption of wireless networks has mushroomed over the last two years. In 2002, only two per cent of UK businesses had a wireless network. Now a third do.

A side effect of this increased connectivity is greater exposure to information security threats. These continue to evolve, with new viruses and vulnerabilities being identified every week. The average UK business now receives roughly 20 viruses a year, and has its website scanned or probed many times. Large businesses are attacked more, receiving on average a virus a week.

At the same time, dependence on electronic information and the systems that process it continues to increase. Eighty seven per cent of UK businesses are now highly dependent compared with 76 per cent two years ago. Over half store highly confidential records on computers. Given this, security breaches are potentially more damaging than ever.

## truth and consequences

As a result, the number of UK businesses that suffer security breaches continues to rise. Sadly, security problems are now a reality for every business, rather than something that happens to someone else. As organisations struggle to contain the threats, the number of security incidents continues to rise.

Malicious incidents are driving this increase. These include viruses, unauthorised access, misuse of systems, fraud and theft. Two thirds of UK businesses have had at least one of these breaches in the last year, compared with only 18 per cent six years ago (DTI Information Security Breaches Survey 2004). The security breaches are not isolated instances. The average UK business now has roughly one security incident a month. Large companies have roughly one a week.

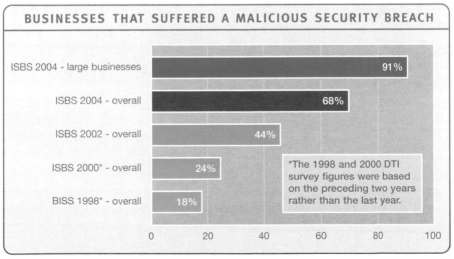

Source: DTI's Information Security Breaches Survey (ISBS)

And the cost is significant. The average cost of an organisation's most serious security incident was roughly £10,000. In large companies, this was more like £120,000. The impact on availability was by far the biggest contributor to this cost, with some organisations suffering a very major disruption to their business operations for more than a month.

What's more, businesses are pessimistic about the future outlook for information security breaches. As expounded by the Jericho Forum, network boundaries are likely to continue to erode, making traditional security defences obsolete. Incidents will happen more often in the future, and will be harder to detect. While the Star Trek experience shows that crystal ball-gazing can be misleading, the picture looks far from rosy.

## view from the top

In the light of this, there is a lot of media attention given to security issues. The newspapers now seem full of stories about teenage hackers and the latest viruses sweeping across the world. Technology providers have hit on security solutions as the latest money-spinner, with sales pitches focused on fear, uncertainty and doubt.

It's important, however, to put this in perspective. Information security is only one of many threats that every business faces. For example, even in the UK banking industry – one of the most security-conscious of sectors – information security is not the highest priority faced by the business. The Centre for the Study of Financial Innovation (CSFI) researches banking risks and ranks them based on their perceived severity. Their latest survey (Banana Skins 2005) shows that while fraud, technology and risk management have all increased significantly as concerns of UK banks over the last two years, none yet make it into the top five. There are bigger issues facing businesses. For banks, overregulation, credit risk, corporate governance, derivatives and hedge funds top the list.

A similar pattern emerges in other industries, such as life assurance or travel, where 9/11 and the stock market fall have threatened business survival. When you're trying to escape a burning house, your attention isn't usually focused on buying a new burglar alarm.

Many sectors have seen cost reduction as a major priority, driving strategic activities such as offshoring and outsourcing. In a cost-constrained environment, justifying extra spend on security is often difficult.

The reality is that information security per se is not normally high on the CEO's priority list. For the major multi-nationals, CEOs' top five concerns (PwC's 8th Annual Global CEO Survey) are overregulation, low-cost competition, oil prices, loss of key talent and market volatility. Only 13 per cent feel that reputational risk is one of the biggest threats to their business, and only eight per cent see intellectual property piracy as a key challenge.

## governance, risk management and compliance

However, just like UK banks, increasingly these global CEOs view governance, risk management and compliance (GRC) as vital to their business. And, it's not just about compliance with laws and regulations. Eighty eight per cent of CEOs agree that effective GRC is a value driver and a source of competitive advantage to their business, whereas only a third focus their GRC solely on laws and regulations.

Effective GRC, therefore, involves identifying the risks that might prevent a business from achieving its objectives and then putting in place strategies for managing those risks. Security threats are becoming increasingly significant, so information security management plays a key role in supporting the GRC of the organisation.

The biggest single concern in most businesses is interruption in service caused by a security incident (such as a virus outbreak). In certain industries (such as financial services), reputational damage is a major concern. In the entertainment, media and pharmaceutical sectors, protection of intellectual property is critical. And, most businesses want to avoid the hassle and bad publicity associated with contravening laws such as the Data Protection Act.

Because GRC is on the CEO's agenda, security has an elevated profile at board level, with the CFO, COO or CIO typically tasked with ensuring these risks are addressed. Three-quarters of respondents to the DTI's Information Security Breaches Survey 2004 rated security as a high or very high priority for their top management or board of directors. The priority is highest in large businesses,

## IS SECURITY SEEN AS A PRIORITY BY SENIOR EXECUTIVES?

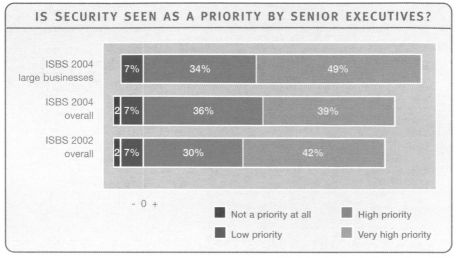

Source: DTI's Information Security Breaches Survey (ISBS)

with five in six considering it important, and in financial services, where every respondent considered it a very high priority.

The message from this is clear. Directors view security as an important component of their overall GRC structures, rather than a business issue in its own right. To be effective, managers responsible for security need to ensure that they communicate security issues in the context of the organisation's overall risk management framework.

## lost in translation

In many businesses, however, there appears to be a gap between the apparent priority given to security and what is done in practice. Three quarters of UK businesses are confident that their technical security processes are sufficient to deal with all significant security breaches (DTI Information Security Breaches Survey 2004). Yet many of these have anti-virus and patching controls that are inadequate in today's environment. Many others have networks that are vulnerable to attack and place excessive reliance on simple – hence breakable – passwords.

One root cause is a skills gap. Some businesses do not fully appreciate the risks they are running, and so think they are safe when they are not. Only one in

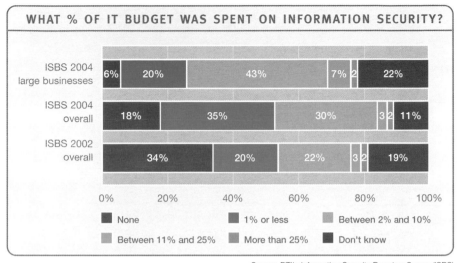

WHAT % OF IT BUDGET WAS SPENT ON INFORMATION SECURITY?

| | None | 1% or less | Between 2% and 10% | Between 11% and 25% | More than 25% | Don't know |
|---|---|---|---|---|---|---|
| ISBS 2004 large businesses | 6% | 20% | 43% | 7% | 2 | 22% |
| ISBS 2004 overall | 18% | 35% | 30% | 3 2 | | 11% |
| ISBS 2002 overall | 34% | 20% | 22% | 3 2 | | 19% |

Source: DTI's Information Security Breaches Survey (ISBS)

ten companies (and only a quarter of large ones) have staff with formal information security qualifications. Relatively few companies have achieved accredited certification to the British Standard for Information Security Management, BS 7799, Part 2 (Specification for an Information Security Management System).

Another cause is that spend on information security, while increasing, is still relatively low. Roughly a quarter of companies appear to be investing appropriate levels in security. In large companies, it is about half. The majority of businesses, however, are still spending less than one per cent of their IT budget on security.

One factor behind the underinvestment is that security is often seen as an overhead rather than an investment. Less than half of all businesses ever evaluate their return on investment (ROI) on security spend. It is not always the case that lack of ROI calculations equates to lack of investment. However, without this information, it can be difficult to prioritise security spend against other projects.

Senior management can also regard security as forced expenditure rather than something that can bring business benefits, particularly where the rationale is not clearly linked to the organisation's overall risk management framework.

Surprisingly, the main reason why businesses do not estimate ROI is that no-one asks for it. This was the case in almost a third of businesses. In a further one in eight companies, the person responsible for information security does not know how to do the calculation. Many of these people come from a technical rather than commercial background, so have never learned the method.

In the organisations that manage security successfully, the board understands the security threats they face sufficiently to hire the expertise they need to address the issues. And, importantly, those security specialists have learned to communicate to the board in business terms, rather than technical jargon.

## five a day

There are some simple steps that businesses of all sizes can take to reduce the likelihood and impact of future security incidents. Based on the results of its Information Security Breaches Survey 2004, the DTI recommends that UK businesses of all sizes:

☐ draw on the right expertise to understand the security threats they face and their legal responsibilities

☐ integrate security into normal business practice, through a clear security policy and staff education

☐ invest appropriately in security controls (to mitigate the risks), or in insurance (to transfer them)

☐ check that their key security defences (such as operating system patches, disaster recovery plans, etc.) are robust and up to date

☐ respond to security incidents efficiently and effectively, to minimise business disruption

Do these five things every day to keep your business healthy.

# main threats to IT security

Threats to IT can come in the form of internal or external attacks. Jeremy Ward, director of Service Development at Symantec, highlights those that are the most common and pernicious

When you walk down an unfamiliar street you are probably alert to threats. By contrast, when you connect to the Internet you most likely feel secure. However, threats posed by the Internet can be as real and potentially damaging as any threat in the street.

The purpose of this chapter is to alert you to some of these threats. The intention is to give you just enough of the 'controlled paranoia' necessary for survival in a potentially hostile environment. But remember, you are not at risk from a threat unless you are both vulnerable to it, and have something that can be exploited by it. Threats should never be looked at in isolation, but always as part of a risk assessment (see chapter 8).

## EXECUTIVE SUMMARY

☐ threats can come from internal, as well as external sources

☐ the virus threat changes and evolves rapidly

☐ criminals can control your system without your knowledge

☐ spam is dangerous as well as a nuisance

☐ criminal use of the Internet is growing rapidly

## the internal threat

It's easy for any company to become fixated on the threat from outside and to neglect internal threats. However, the most ubiquitous threat to IT security is the internal user. The threat is real and constant, as more security incidents are found consistently to come from inside an organisation as outside, according to the CSI/FBI Computer Crime and Security Survey 2004. Such internal risks might originate from simple errors and omissions when entering data – more likely with new employees – particularly following the introduction of new applications and software.

A recent study in the US – Ponemon Institute's Survey on Data Security Breaches, February 2005 – showed that the leading cause of data security breaches (39 per cent) was employee error.

A frequently encountered example is when individuals who are unfamiliar with the system send emails to incorrect or inappropriate addressees. Although the consequences may be trivial, in the past such mistakes have resulted in costly litigation and damage to a company's reputation.

Deliberate internal fraud or malicious acts using IT systems are more difficult to identify, particularly if the perpetrator is expert and skilled. However, experience has shown that the threat increases in proportion to the number of short-term IT contracting staff employed by a company. The threat also rises during times of internal restructuring and during mergers and acquisitions.

---

### BEWARE THE CONSULTANT

In 2003 a consultant working for two major IT security suppliers was arrested while manning a stand at an IT security show in London.

It turned out that the security firms had unwittingly employed the man accused of being the brains behind the infamous 'Fluffi Bunni' hacking group.

---

## viruses, worms and Trojan Horses

When considering IT threats, viruses are probably the first thing that comes to mind. For 10 years they have had a high profile in the media, due to the damage and disruption they cause to millions of computers all over the world.

Viruses have consistently taken the top spot in surveys of reported security breaches, such as the FBI Computer Crime and Security Survey and the DTI's Information Security Breaches Survey 2004, where viruses were the top-rated problem cited by 78 per cent and 50 per cent of respondents, respectively.

You will often hear the terms 'worm' and 'Trojan Horses' mentioned in the same context as computer viruses. Both of these are a type of computer virus. A worm is computer code that, like an ordinary virus, attaches itself to existing 'good' code, after which it creates multiple copies of itself. These copies are able to propagate through your system or to be sent to other systems.

Like the original from which it was named, a Trojan Horse is a piece of computer software that appears to be benevolent – perhaps a screen saver or a game – but contains potentially dangerous code. This may open a 'backdoor' into your system, enabling the hacker to take control of your computer without your knowledge. Or it may capture information about what you are typing on your computer and send it back to its originator.

Viruses, worms and Trojan Horses can be grouped under the term 'malicious software'. This is used in the abbreviated form of 'malware' throughout the rest of this chapter.

## parasite

Computer malware is parasitic. It can't exist without a host (your software). As such, it has to meet certain requirements to ensure its success. Among these are that it needs to:

☐ spread rapidly and efficiently

☐ get through its host's defences

☐ survive inside its host without being destroyed

☐ extract sustenance from its host – preferably without destroying it too soon

Early on, the hackers who devised computer malware learned how to make their creations spread. They use email that tricks recipients into opening a file that downloads the malware, usually by promising that the file contains an attractive image. The malware then copies and sends itself to every person on the recipient's email address list.

Such 'mass mailing' malware is a nuisance since it can easily produce a flood of emails that will overwhelm a company's email system. It can also be actively damaging if it also contains, for example, instructions to wipe all the information contained on the host's hard drive. That said, very few pieces of malware now have these overtly damaging actions, since destroying the host will lead to their own demise.

In themselves mass mailers are not successful parasites, as they can be stopped by some simple defences. As a result, hackers have rapidly developed malware that propagates without needing an attachment. Just opening the email triggers the malicious action. Some other types of malware block anti-virus systems, and other types actively change themselves so that they won't be recognised as malicious by the anti-virus mechanism. And, as fast as efforts increase to stop them, they continue to evolve.

However, such malware does not necessarily meet the requirement to survive without being destroyed by its host. To do this, a virus can remain dormant for months, or even years. In this state it will be difficult to detect and eliminate. Once it has evaded destruction, it may be activated remotely by a hacker, using a 'backdoor'. When an attacker has gained control of your computer it is said to have been turned into a 'robot' or 'bot'.

It is these qualities, along with others, that enable malware to meet the fourth requirement of a successful parasite. Hackers are increasingly connecting these 'bots' into networks ('botnets') that can be used for a number of criminal purposes.

## spam, phishing and identity theft

One such crime is when hackers instruct their botnets to send spam. This is often seen as a mere nuisance, but can be far more damaging. The sheer volume of spam can overwhelm business systems and swamp genuine communication. In September 2004, 66 per cent of all Internet email was spam.

Far more significantly, spam can also be used to transmit malware and as a medium for committing fraud; in the UK in October 2004, nine per cent of spam was fraudulent and eight per cent contained scams of one kind or another.

The 'phishing' attack is the most recent, and successful, type of fraud that is committed using spam. What happens is that the victim will receive an email

## SPAM AND PHISHING VOLUMES

In September 2004, a large US bank was the victim of 150 different types of phishing and fraud attacks. It received 5,200,000 fraudulent and phishing emails and is now blocking more than 500,000 emails a day.

message that appears to be a genuine communication from their bank, or a business that they have used online. The message may indicate that the recipient needs to take action to protect themselves from fraud by logging onto the company's website and entering some details. A link may be provided to a site that looks genuine. The bogus site may ask for details of the victim's account and credit card details. These will then be gathered by the criminal.

When such details have been stolen, the target will have become one of the increasing number of victims of 'identity theft'. The criminal can go on to use the stolen identity to defraud other companies, to launder money and commit other crimes. By association, any company whose website is spoofed will also be damaged by its unwitting association with a fraudulent attack.

## denial of service attacks

The 'denial of service' attack is a simple concept: a hacker swamps a company's online business with fraudulent messages that make it unable to respond to genuine business users. Criminals can launch such attacks by using conventional mass mailing malware, or by using an army of botnets. Such attacks have been launched by social activists against companies they felt were behaving unethically, or by those with a grudge against a company, such as a disgruntled former employee or even customer.

However, 2004 witnessed a new development in the use of denial of service attacks by criminal gangs. Such gangs have threatened to launch an attack against a company with a significant online business unless they are paid protection money. Such extortion attempts have been particularly targeted against online gambling sites. Some companies have paid up, judging it better to lose some money to extortion than the millions of pounds it might have cost them in lost business.

## RUSSIAN ROULETTE

In July 2004, the UK National Hi-Tech Crime Unit, working with the Russian police, arrested a gang in Russia responsible for using denial of service attacks against online gambling businesses in the UK.

One UK company was reported to be losing up to £1m a day in business following attacks, and more than a dozen offshore gambling sites serving the US were also attacked. Attacks were timed to coincide with major sporting events, so as to cause maximum disruption.

## don't despair

Although the threat to IT security may seem huge, and growing, all is not lost. There are some simple fixes that businesses can adopt to protect themselves and minimise the vulnerabilities that make them open to threat. These are covered in the next chapter.

# putting IT defences in place

> **There are a number of fundamental defence measures every business should implement, says Jeremy Ward director of Service Development at Symantec**

The last chapter outlined some of the major IT-related threats. Broadly, these fall into two types: those that originate inside your organisation, and those that come from outside. In this chapter we will look at the defences you need, and how to strengthen the measures you already have in place to help reduce the risks from both types of threat. We are not concerned with physical defences, as it is assumed that most businesses will have adequate measures already in place. (Business continuity is dealt with in chapter 4.)

## personnel security

Good personnel security is the best defence against internal IT-related threats. Verification checks on employees needn't be costly or resource intensive. Remember, you are just as vulnerable (or more so) from temporary and contract staff so you should ask for the same verification from them. It's also worth investigating whether the agency you employ carries out these checks. (Ask to see proof.)

Also remember that dismissal can be more dangerous than recruitment. You should have clear procedures to make sure that dismissed former employees have no opportunity to steal vital company information or damage your IT systems before or after they leave. (Further information about personnel security issues is contained in chapter 9.)

## security awareness

Security awareness is probably the most significant single defence measure that any company can institute against both internal and external threats. Again, there is no need for this to be elaborate. Employees and contractors need to be made aware that, as a company, you intend to protect the security of the information – about customers, suppliers and employees – that you hold and use. Everyone needs to play a part in this.

## security policy and procedures

Your security policy, and the procedures that flow from it, should be written down and reviewed regularly. Everyone should see the policy and procedures and be trained in them. Such training doesn't need to be lengthy or complicated, and can even be conducted online through your IT network. However, it needs to be kept up. Frequent reminders should be issued and re-training undertaken regularly.

ood security policies and procedures are the foundation of security aware-ness and of strong defence against threats to your information systems. Even a small company will benefit from a short statement of policy and a few basic security procedures. Further details can be found in chapter 7.

## fixing software vulnerabilities

The malware threats discussed in chapter 2 are able to pose a risk because they can exploit vulnerabilities in people and procedures. They are also able to exploit software vulnerabilities. These are flaws in programming that can allow unauthorised access to, or interference with, a computer system.

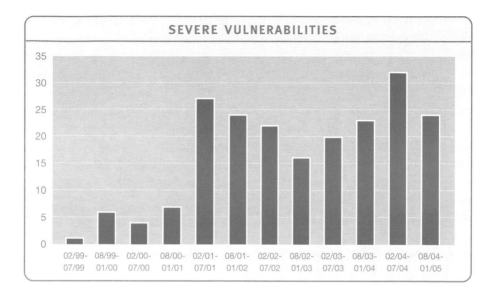

SEVERE VULNERABILITIES

Severe vulnerabilities are those software flaws that can potentially make the greatest impact on a business, depending on the ease with which they can be exploited and their ability to provide increased privileges and access to more prominent targets. They have the potential to cause widespread and serious damage to the information running on those applications that are vulnerable.

The rate at which these severe vulnerabilities are discovered is on the increase. The chart above is taken from the Symantec DeepSight Alerting System, and shows the rising number of severe vulnerabilities discovered between February 1999 and January 2005.

The cure for these vulnerabilities is to apply a 'patch'. This is a piece of code that is released by the software vendor and can be downloaded from the Internet. However, it is unfortunate that the time available to patch these high impact vulnerabilities before they are exploited by a malware threat is continually decreasing. According to the Symantec Internet Security Threat Report of September 2004, the average time is now less than six days.

Many small businesses have fewer problems in patching than larger organisations because they run fewer applications and operating systems and don't need to test new patches as they're released by the software vendor. They also have fewer issues about stopping and re-booting their systems once a patch has been applied. The trick for the small business is to be alert to the need for patching and to remember to download relevant patches every week. Some software offer a 'live update' facility that will automatically do this for you, at an interval you specify, when you are connected to the Internet.

## technical defences

Even a system that has up-to-date patches, is used by people with good security awareness and that has effective security procedures will require technical defences against IT-related threats. Unfortunately, this can be a highly specialised subject. However, anyone who uses an IT system should be aware of the basics, and every company that uses the Internet in its business should ensure that the fundamental technical defence measures are in place. The three basic building blocks of Internet-related technical defence are:

☐   access, authentication and authorisation controls

☐   anti-virus and content-filtering systems

☐   firewalls and network defences

Other mechanisms, such as cryptography and intrusion detection and prevention, are probably inappropriate for most small and medium-sized enterprises, as these require the services of a specialised IT department. Businesses that use wireless networks will require special precautions, as will those with remote and home users (see chapter 6).

## access, authorisation and authentication

Most small businesses do not need to employ complex and costly access, authorisation and authentication controls for their IT systems. However, any business needs to ensure that the access it allows its employees is:

☐   appropriate for the job

☐   removed when no longer required

☐   given only to those applications that employees need to do their jobs

### PASSWORD TIPS

☐ passwords should not be obvious – names or birth dates, 'admin' or 'password' – but be made up of letters – both upper and lower case – numbers and special keys, and be six or more characters in length

☐ it helps to consider your password as a memorable phrase, not a single word. For example: "At forty two, I'm a star" could be written as: @42Ima*!

☐ passwords shouldn't be written down for anyone to find – under the keyboard on a Post-it note – for example

☐ passwords shouldn't be shared between employees, as this will interfere with the audit trail if anything goes wrong

☐ passwords should be changed regularly, say, every three months

Ideally, you should also ensure that you keep a record of who has had access to your critical information, and when they had it.

The most effective mechanism is to enforce a good password control procedure. Most software applications make it easy for you to implement a password and enable you to enforce rules about what the password looks like, and how often it is changed. See the box above for tips on passwords. It is particularly important when installing any application that can be accessed from the Internet to make sure you change the default password.

## anti-virus and content filtering systems

According to the DTI's Information Security Breaches Survey 2004, virtually all businesses now use some form of anti-virus software. The important feature of anti-virus systems is that they need to be updated constantly if they are to go on protecting you. In its Internet Security Threat Report of March 2005, Symantec documented 7,360 new viruses and worms that targeted Windows operating systems and applications between August 2004 and January 2005; this represented an increase of 64% over the previous six-month period. That's about 40 new viruses every day. An anti-virus system that isn't updated becomes increasingly useless. Fortunately, most anti-virus systems offer you the option of automatically downloading updates whenever you are online. Small businesses should always opt for these automatic

## TOP TEN TIPS FOR SMALL AND MEDIUM-SIZED BUSINESSES

The following constitute the essentials of defence for your IT security:

☐ carrying out basic screening checks on all your employees and contractors

☐ having short, clearly documented security policies and procedures

☐ carrying out basic security awareness training with your employees

☐ implementing patches for software vulnerabilities as soon as possible

☐ knowing who is accessing your systems, and why

☐ using strong passwords and changing them regularly

☐ making sure your anti-virus system is updated every few days

☐ using a content-filtering system to guard against spam and phishing

☐ using a firewall, especially if you have broadband Internet access

☐ using an 'all-in-one' network defence system with a small network

See chapter 7 for more on SMEs

downloads – any associated risks are far, far smaller than those associated with getting a virus infection.

Content filtering is important to weed out spam and phishing attacks (see chapter 2). It may take a little effort to 'train' a content-filtering system, to ensure that it does not take out legitimate emails. However, any business with a lot of email traffic, and a strong Internet presence, is well advised to implement content filtering.

## firewalls and network defences

A firewall is essential for any business that has a broadband connection to the Internet. Firewalls are inexpensive software devices that can easily be installed on any computer that has Internet access. They are the best defence against the Trojan Horse malware discussed in chapter 2. Experiments have shown that a computer with broadband Internet access, and without a firewall, can become infected within six minutes of going online.

Some new operating systems have installed a firewall as an integrated feature. Firewalls are essentially 'gatekeepers' that decide what can be let through, and what should be blocked. Any good firewall will come with a set of pre-determined 'policies' that enables it to carry out these gate-keeping duties. Modifying these policies is a highly technical matter, and should not be attempted by an amateur.

Network defences can combine anti-virus, content filtering and firewalls into a single system. This often includes an intrusion detection system, to alert you to possible attack. These systems can come ready-loaded onto a single hardware box to be plugged into your network at the 'gateway' between it and the Internet. Such systems should be considered if you have a small, Internet-linked network as they can save you administrative time and effort.

Always remember, there is no single 'magic bullet' for IT security – and no substitute for good security awareness and procedures.

# DTI
# UK
# ISO/IEC 17799
# Users' Group

The UK ISO/IEC 17799 Users' Group is an industry led forum with the business mission of promoting and disseminating the exchange of best practice and knowledge of good information security management from ISO/IEC 17799 and its companion standard BS 7799 Part 2. The UK Users' Group provides companies with the opportunity to discuss with others how to apply and use the best practice given in these standards.

The UK Users' Group runs a number of workshops each year. These allow organisations to get together to learn and discuss with those that are already using these standards. These events also allow members to network with one another. Previous events have covered topics such as:

- Outsourcing and external service provision
- Incident handling
- Data protection and the Freedom of Information Act
- Certification
- Risk assessment

The UK Users' Group is also linked to the ISMS International User Group (ISMSIUG@aol.com) providing Members with access to a global network of information security best practice.

For further information about this group or to obtain an application form please contact the UK Users' Group Secretariat:

Information Security Policy Team
Department of Trade and Industry
151 Buckingham Palace Road
London SW1W 9SS
Tel:      020 7215 1962
Fax:      020 7215 1966
email:    isoiec17799usersgroup@dti.gsi.gov.uk
web:      www.dti.gov.uk/industries/information_security

dti

# the value of business continuity

Effective business continuity is still eluding many businesses. Andrew Beard, director of Performance Improvement Consulting at PricewaterhouseCoopers LLP, stresses the importance of getting it right

Business continuity is an ongoing issue, but it received renewed attention in the wake of the bombings of 11 September 2001. Many organisations revisited their own contingency plans and the UK government raised not only its own game, but also that of the companies providing services considered part of the UK's critical infrastructure.

The impact is already being seen. In the financial services sector the regulator, the Financial Services Authority (FSA), has already been involved in co-ordinating industry-wide simulation exercises. The focus of regulatory authorities, together with the ever-increasing expectations of customers and suppliers for business availability, provide compelling reasons for making sure continuity plans are robust.

## EXECUTIVE SUMMARY

- ☐ the starting point is to identify what activities are critical to running the business
- ☐ business continuity is as much about process as technology
- ☐ senior management must show its commitment and support
- ☐ it is essential that any individual designated to manage your business continuity has sufficient authority to do so effectively

However, business continuity remains a significant challenge for many organisations. It seems to have a language all of its own, where 'RPOs' and 'RTOs' need to be applied to 'MCAs' and few are clear on the difference between business continuity plans, business continuity management and crisis management. This chapter aims to stick to plain English. It will examine some of the key business continuity challenges and offer practical advice on how to ensure that critical business systems stay up and running and can be recovered efficiently in the event of an incident.

## challenges for the smaller business

So, what are the challenges for UK organisations, particularly for those whose size does not permit the luxury of external consulting advice, or a dedicated internal business continuity management capability?

The first important area is to understand what activities are critical to running the business. This can be done through an exercise often referred to as business impact analysis (BIA). This is an identification process driven by analysing the impacts of a disruption to critical activities. Additionally, the BIA will help identify the critical systems. These activities – often referred to as mission critical activities (MCAs) – will vary depending on the type of organisation. For example, for organisations such as E-bay and Amazon, the availability of the company website is critical as without it they cannot trade. By contrast, a small manufacturer of machine parts is less likely to feel that the loss of its website represents a short-term threat to its business.

Failure to perform a BIA effectively can lead to wasted time and money in recovering non-critical processes and systems and delays in recovering those that are critical to the business.

## the importance of processes

Having identified the most important systems and processes, organisations need to make sure that such systems are designed to be resilient, and in the event of a failure, that they can be recovered with minimal disruption to the business. It is important to recognise that business continuity is not just about technology. Without a full plan covering business processes as well as technology, the ability to recover business activities in the event of a disaster will be impaired.

One example, seen at several organisations, is that key business data is backed up on a regular basis and sent away from the main computer site. Staff may also be provided with pagers or mobile phones for contact purposes. However, many companies fail to recognise that they may not be able to make contact immediately.

Another common mistake is to underestimate the time that is required to physically get staff to a recovery site. One organisation had plans that assumed that the restoration of its data could begin within one hour of the recovery plan being invoked. This was despite the fact that the recovery site was a minimum of two hours' travel for the support staff and that the backup media were also stored over two hours away from the recovery site. The impact was that the plan, if invoked at six o'clock on a week day morning would not, in reality, allow the process of data recovery to begin until at least 10 o'clock. The organisation's recovery plans were based on being able to recover critical systems by nine o'clock. Assumptions such as these are one of the most common failings of business continuity management.

## keeping backups off site

Worryingly, it seems that many organisations are not even getting the basics right. The DTI's Backups and Recovery fact sheet – part of its 2004 Information Security Breaches Survey – noted that only a third of businesses store their backups off site.

Another cornerstone of effective business continuity is to assign one person as responsible, with support from senior management. This is often missing in organisations; because of its importance business continuity needs the full support of senior management. It is not enough to appoint someone as a business continuity co-ordinator unless they are sufficiently empowered to make decisions and are able to secure the necessary investment and commitment from management.

The selection of individuals to perform business continuity co-ordination is another important consideration. It is sometimes argued that business continuity is a matter of common sense. There may be an element of truth in this. However, effective continuity plans are far more likely to be developed by experienced professionals.

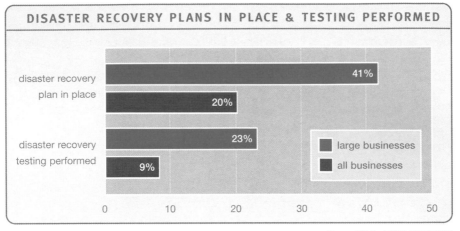

DISASTER RECOVERY PLANS IN PLACE & TESTING PERFORMED

Source: DTI April 2004 URN 04/610

## testing your recovery plan

Perhaps the most common area of business continuity failure relates to recovery plans and, in particular, the degree of testing. According to the Backups and recovery fact sheet, 41 per cent of large organisations have plans in place, yet only 23 per cent test those plans. Among all UK companies the figures are even more worrying, with just 20 per cent having plans and only eight per cent performing testing of the plans.

## key steps to getting started

So, what practical steps can organisations take to ensure that a crisis does not become a catastrophe? The following are some 'starter' points that organisations should consider.

First, recognise the importance of business continuity. UK companies report that they find it easy to make a business case for spending on backups and disaster recovery. This is encouraging news but, as already illustrated, business continuity goes beyond backups.

Organisations that already have continuity plans should review them on a regular basis and consider the use of business continuity experts as part of the review. Companies that have not yet developed plans should also seek expert advice. A good starting point is the Business Continuity Institute website, www.thebci.org. The site provides information about general management issues and also provides links to good practice BCM documents, including the Publicly Available Specification (PAS) 56.

Second, work out what is most at risk. Identify the systems, and individuals on which the company's business depends most. The information can be used to drive both resilience and recovery. Core IT systems should not only be recoverable, but designed and implemented to minimise the risk of disruption. For example, at a technical level the risk of a single computer failure can be minimised by the use of dual processors and disk storage based on RAID (redundant array of inexpensive risks – disk failure is the number one cause of 'downtime').

Third, develop a strategy. A business continuity strategy should consider items such as risk appetite, use of third parties for recovery, 'failover' capabilities between geographically diverse centres and the creation of 'zones' to support failover capabilities.

Fourth, create, maintain and test recovery plans. Plans are vital to minimising the impact of disruptive events. They should be agreed on and all involved should be consulted. But plans have no value if they are not tested regularly, so it is important to include a schedule of tests as part of any plan. Tests should reflect plausible disruptive threats. They should focus on the most likely threats first and then add more complex and less likely scenarios over a period of time. Avoid 'shelf-ware' plans. Make them work and keep them up to date by engaging the business management in the tests and in the maintenance process.

Finally, don't forget about people. Organisations are prone to overlooking both the impact of individuals not being available and the practical aspects of where they will be located in the event of an existing location being unavailable for an extended period of time.

You may have missed that 13-19 March 2005 was International Business Continuity week (see www.thebci.org). Hopefully those that did take note had a timely reminder to shake the dust off their existing plans, reassess their relevance and quality and make sure there are schedules to test effectiveness. But don't wait for next March, or the one after, to do the same.

**7799 Goes Global**
ISMS International
User Group

Information Security Management
# Ten Years of Best Practice
London, 12-13th Dec 2005

This year will see the publication of the revised version of ISO/IEC 17799 and this happens to coincide with the 10 year anniversary from when the first BS 7799 Code of Practice was published back in February 1995. Over these past ten years the business world has had an opportunity to apply this best practice in many fields and the international response to its adoption has been staggering. Today ISO/IEC 17799 is known around the world as the common language for information security best practice. Also this year it is expected the number of certificates will continue to rise, well surpassing the striking rate of growth we have seen in 2004. Furthermore, developments in the international standards arena will see the emergence of the ISO version of BS 7799 Part 2 and the progress of a standard covering ISMS metrics and measurements to measure the effectiveness of information security.

This year's UK 7799 Goes Global will celebrate the first ten years of 7799 with an impressive line-up of lively and informative presentations of the Past, Present and Future developments: What have trends been in the threats, risks, business applications and processes? How have these shaped the exciting new development emerging from ISO? What are the challenges organisations have experienced and what best practice solutions have been implemented to deal with these? How can these ISMS standards help to meet compliance requirements? These and many more hot topics will feature at this year's event.

FURTHER INFORMATION
To obtain further information about this event contact:

**ISMS International User Group**: Ted Humphreys (tedxisec@aol.com) or Angelika Plate (aexis@aol.com) or visit the Events page of the web www.xisec.com
**DTI Information Security Policy Team:** infosecpolicyteam@dti.gsi.gov.uk

**Corporate Sponsors**

**Supported by**

Symantec    KPMG Deutsche Treuhand Gesellschaft AG

*Be sure not to miss this event of the year – network with other users, hear the latest from those involved in these important international developments in standards, certification and governance and regulatory compliance.*

# the ecommerce challenge

> **The fast pace of change in the world of online trading demands extra vigilance from companies, says Jon Fell, partner at law firm Pinsent Masons**

Ecommerce is the transaction of business online. As such, it includes all transactions entered into electronically, whether by email or via a website. Further, ecommerce covers not only consumer transactions, but also includes transactions between businesses. While the security issues relating to the different means of communication and the concerns of each of the parties may be different, there are common themes. It is essential for each party to know:

☐ the identity of the person they are dealing with

☐ that the information on which they are both relying has not been tampered with during transmission

☐ that once received, the information will be kept secure by the recipient

In order to manage the security of online transactions a business must first identify and understand the risks.

**EXECUTIVE SUMMARY**

☐ any business wanting to trade online must factor in security at the planning stage

☐ online trading risks can be split into two categories: commercial and legal

☐ organisational issues have just as much impact on security as technical issues

## authentication

There are two aspects to authentication. First, there is the authentication of an individual user. It is very difficult to know who you're dealing with online. Most transactions are based on an element of trust. This is particularly true when purchasing from a website. The person buying online will take comfort from the reputation of the business and the use of secure web technology. When contracting by email thought should be given to the importance of verifying the identity of the individual sending the email. If it is decided that this is of vital importance, then consideration may be given to the use of digital signatures.

The second aspect of authentication is in relation to the data itself. Both the sender and the recipient have a keen interest in ensuring that the data has not been altered during transmission, nor after it has been received. Typically, this is achieved by means of encryption technology and ensuring that the data is stored in a secure environment with a complete audit trail showing accesses and changes to the data. This is particularly important in relation to personal data where there is a legal obligation to put in place appropriate security (see also chapter 10).

## identifying the risks

The risks associated with online trading can be split into two broad categories: commercial and legal. Commercial risks range from the obvious danger of not being paid or being the victim of a scam, to the potential damage to your reputation if your systems are breached. Often the direct consequences pale into insignificance compared with the damage to an organisation's reputation. The fact that its systems were breached tends to be remembered far longer than the facts relating to that breach or the way in which the organisation reacted. Some of the legal risks associated with electronic trading have been identified in chapter 10.

Once the risks have been analysed, the business will need to devise a plan to minimise any threats and implement it. However, all too often a business focuses on the technical steps that can be taken to protect the data rather than the organisational ones. They are of equal importance.

## some specific risks

In order to protect itself, a business needs to identify where risks may arise and then evaluate those risks. Set out below are some examples of the typical risks faced by a business trading electronically:

- capacity. It may be essential to know who you are dealing with because of the nature of the goods and services that you are providing, or due to the authority of the particular individual you are dealing with in the organisation. Unless you know who they are, and the level to which their authority extends, you may not be able to enforce a contract

- phishing. These are emails that are sent from scammers, purporting to be a legitimate service provider, asking for details of a user's accounts, passwords and personal identification numbers. At present, the main targets are banks and credit card companies. These financial institutions are accepting liability currently. However, this may well change with the growth in phishing attacks. The terms and conditions of use of online banking facilities and credit cards require the user to keep their passwords and identification details secret. By disclosing these to a third party, the terms will be breached and the financial institution will be entitled to decline to accept responsibility

- pharming. There is a disturbing new form of identity scam known as pharming, which is a form of domain name spoofing and takes place at the local domain name server level. The user sees what he believes is the genuine site with the correct URL, but has in fact been diverted to a scam site. One way of combating this is with the use of digital certificates on web pages. This allows the user to check the authenticity of the site. The problem is that most users know little, if anything, about digital certificates

- credit card fraud. One of the biggest problems for any online business is that of credit card fraud. The credit card industry has taken steps to provide additional levels of security by the use of personal identification numbers. While this may be effective in reducing fraud where the card holder is present, there is a risk that there will be an increase in online credit fraud. The problem facing a retailer is that the risk of fraud lies with it and not with the holder of the credit card. Unless the retailer signs up to a verification scheme, such as those operated by Visa and MasterCard, the credit card companies oblige the retailer to repay any funds that have been received by the retailer in the event that the transaction is fraudulent. However, there are two main problems with such verification services. First, they add an extra step in the online retail process. Second, they require the customer to have signed up with the service. It is essential that a business takes all the steps that it can to ensure that it knows with whom it is dealing and that the credit card is being used in a lawful manner

## managing the risk

There are a number of steps that a business can take to manage online risks. These will be determined by carrying out a risk analysis. The following are some basic steps that can any business can take to protect its position:

☐ development stage. It is essential that when a new website is developed, it is designed and developed with security in mind. It is much easier to incorporate security into the site as it is built rather than adding it at the end. This is one of the points that should be specifically dealt with in the agreement between a business and its web developer

☐ terms and conditions. There are a number of ways in which terms and conditions can be used to protect a business selling online. The key ones relate to supply of goods or services by the business. In these, the business can seek to apportion liability between the supplier and the customer, and can also include warranties as to identity and capacity. Equally, use of disclaimers and notices on a site can help to reduce liability in relation to content or representations that may have been made. While the use of terms and conditions in itself will not provide an absolute protection, it does play an essential part in the management of online risk

☐ external security. Most businesses have their websites hosted by third parties. It is important to ensure that those third parties have in place appropriate security in relation to the physical and electronic access to the servers on which the website is stored

☐ business continuity. One of the key aspects of any secure system is to ensure that the data has been backed up in a way that is easy to restore and to identify any particular items of data

☐ review. The most important point to bear in mind about any form of security is that it should not be static. It is necessary for a business to review the risks regularly as they will change over a period. This in turn will require a review of the security that has been put in place

# managing mobile and wireless risks

Mobile and wireless communications make the boundary of your network porous, says Peter Judge, business and technology writer

Letting your staff access email and other mobile data on the move sounds like a good idea, but what are the downsides? The biggest one is probably the security risks.

Mobile access makes it easier for your staff to get data – but it also opens up the possibility of other people accessing it. You may think it would be more secure to prevent mobile access, and keep your data on your own physical network. This would mean that other people would have to get into your office building and connect to your network in order to get at your private information.

But, even if you don't allow remote connections, your data is already moving in and out of the office, on laptops and personal digital assistants (PDAs). And those devices are vulnerable. They get left around, and they get compromised. Nearly 6,000 PDAs and 5,000 laptops were left in London taxi cabs during a six-month period, according to a survey by mobile security vendor Pointsec and the London cabbie's journal, *Taxi*.

## EXECUTIVE SUMMARY

- [ ] remote working makes employees more powerful, but creates risks, by opening your network boundary

- [ ] a sound policy is the cornerstone to secure mobility, not piecewise technical 'fixes'

- [ ] passwords, virtual private networks (VPNs) and encryption are the basic IT building blocks for security

- [ ] don't stick your head in the sand – a policy that 'forbids' remote working may be the most dangerous of all

"Talk to your IT department," says Magnus Ahlberg, managing director of Pointsec. "Legislation is slowly becoming more specific in this arena and there is a good chance we will soon see legal action taken against individuals and organisations that do not protect information that they store on other people."

## building a policy

Since mobility is happening, you need to plan for it so that you get the benefits with the minimum of risk. It's important to get both users and your IT department to determine what mobile access you need. Only then can you identify the risks. Essential questions to ask users are:

☐ what applications do they want access to, eg. email, ERP, CRM, other back-end software?

☐ where do they need access? At home, on the road, or at hotspots?

☐ what equipment will they carry around, eg. laptops, PDAs, smartphones?

Essential questions to ask IT are:

☐ what applications can they secure?

☐ what devices can they support?

☐ what connection methods can they work with – GPRS, Wi-Fi, 3G?

☐ what level of support can they provide?

The policy should then be worked out on the basis of those answers.

Once you know what kind of mobile access you are going to offer, you will need to identify the right tools to secure it.

## always encrypt and use passwords

Data on mobile devices can be easily accessible if the device falls into the wrong hands. To prevent this, encrypt the information stored on laptops, and make sure that users have to enter a password every time a laptop starts up, and every time they use a corporate PDA.

## ACTION PLAN

- ☐ develop a policy that addresses human behaviour before you decide on what technology you want
- ☐ ensure employees know the policy and understand the consequences of flouting it
- ☐ don't forget physical security. The biggest risk to data on PDAs or laptops is when the equipment is lost or stolen
- ☐ to minimise the need for patches and updates concentrate on a small number of standardised products and services
- ☐ when a remote user connects, authenticate the user (as well as the machine, if possible)
- ☐ encrypt data on devices, and use VPNs to make a secure link for all remote connections
- ☐ use public Wi-Fi, but use it with care
- ☐ manage mobile devices centrally, even if it means buying a specialist product to control kit used at home
- ☐ don't ignore mobility. A policy that forbids mobile access will require expensive vigilance, and still leave you open to trouble from unauthorised 'grey' links

Data in transit can be intercepted, especially if it's going over a wireless link, such as the GPRS (cellphone data) network or a Wi-Fi connection. It is best to assume that any network outside your office is insecure.

Virtual private networks (VPNs) are a well-tested way to get data across an untrusted link. These encrypt all the data at one end, and decode it at the other, creating a sort of encrypted 'tunnel' between the two devices. Most mobile devices can run VPN software, so make sure that your IT department can set up a VPN and support the different devices in use.

Obviously, the fewer devices involved the better. The more you have, the more security work for your IT department, and the greater the chance of a leak. Every mobile device is susceptible to weaknesses, and these will need to be patched from time to time.

In particular, smartphones vary tremendously, and handset manufacturers are well known for changing their portfolio. Adopting one of these phones may mean that two years down the line you are supporting security on a platform that its manufacturer views as obsolete.

VPNs need to authenticate the user as well as the machine, to make sure that the connection is not being used by an untrusted person who has, say, stumbled across a laptop by chance.

## watch out for Wi-Fi

Wireless networks (Wi-Fi) have had a lot of security attention, with relevant security standards continually changing, and regular 'scares' occurring. At the time of writing, the most recent of these scares was the 'Evil Twin' attack, whereby a hacker set up a wireless laptop to mimic a public hotspot and suckered users to log on and hand over their passwords. However, this kind of attack has been known about for some time and is unlikely to become a reality. The best way to protect yourself is to use a VPN, and to favour private wireless networks to public ones.

Users should not assume public wired connections are more secure. Terminals in Internet cafes can have keyboard loggers installed, or caches that get checked after your user has left, which makes virtually all traffic vulnerable.

## central control

A number of products exist that are designed to manage and control a fleet of mobile systems. These should be able to do the following jobs:

- ☐ distribute security updates and patches

- ☐ enforce encryption on the device, including any removable storage

- ☐ vet the mobile device for any viruses it has picked up while outside corporate control

- ☐ remotely shut down – and preferably wipe clean – any device remotely that has been lost or stolen

## security at home

In some cases, the majority of a company's remote workers are based at home. This can be easier to control than 'true' remote working as it enables businesses to mandate the kind of hardware employees use. But, home use does present its own potential problems. The user's broadband connection will more than likely be shared by his or her family and/or housemates. Ideally, work machines should be kept separate from home machines that are sharing the broadband connection. It's also important to ensure the work machine has relevant software to guard against spyware, Trojans and viruses.

## don't hold back

You cannot ignore mobile access and any attempt to do so may cause the biggest security risk of all. There are products that your staff can install, which allow a mobile phone to control and access a desktop PC, even inside your corporate firewall. One of the most powerful of these is Sproqit, which allows the phone to browse any computer on the network, and receive and send email, while on the move.

Because these products are out there, you can guarantee that your staff will be setting up their own mobile access, if you do not provide it in a secure and controlled way.

There are real security risks in mobile working but they are manageable. The benefits are also real, so a wise business will proceed, having taken all possible precautions.

# CHAPTER 7

# IT security for the SME

Angus McIlwraith, senior consultant at Insight Consulting, outlines some low-cost high-value practical measures that smaller businesses can adopt to protect themselves

Dedicated technical staff are expensive, and many smaller companies cannot afford such specialist staff full time. Obtaining information and IT security specialists is probably more expensive, and consultancy rates are high and do not always offer good value to the SME.

## EXECUTIVE SUMMARY

- [ ] most lapses in security are a result of human error or misunderstanding
- [ ] don't leave your expensive equipment out on display
- [ ] restrict the facilities you give to staff to those they need to do their job
- [ ] take proper precautions when disposing of sensitive information

That's the bad news. The good news is that there are a number of straightforward, sensible actions you can take that will demonstrably decrease the risks you face when managing your IT investment, as well as to the information that you use to operate your business. Most of these actions are cyclical and should form part of your routine business process. The frequency with which you perform these tasks varies – some might need to be done once a week, some each month and others only once a year.

The first action you should take is to perform a risk analysis. Look at each of your various business processes and determine what unwelcome events (eg. a fire) would have the most impact in terms of loss. In this context, 'loss' could include loss of revenue, direct replacement of hardware, or litigation against your company for failing to deliver. Once you know which events would potentially be most damaging, you need to apply controls, either to prevent them from happening, or to reduce the impact of such events. You should also develop controls to inform you of an unwanted event, and to provide a means of recovering from its impact should it manifest.

Risk analysis can be a highly specialist subject (see also chapter 8). The following controls are those most likely to help SMEs in the most likely scenarios.

## backing up

Take backup copies of your most important information and programs. This is fairly straightforward for computer-based information, but is more difficult for paper files. Backing up should be done regularly, on a frequency that is often best determined by your business cycle, or by your risk analysis process. One way of thinking about it is to determine how much information you are prepared to lose before deciding on how regularly you perform the backing up process.

Keep the backed up information physically separate from the original, and make sure that the staff who need to recover the information in the event of some catastrophe know where it is kept.

If you have very important paper documents, keep them in a fireproof safe or something similar. Even a locked cupboard can provide considerable protection against flames, smoke and even the damage caused by water from fire hoses.

## physical security

Keep your offices and other premises physically secure. If you can, make sure you know who is in your premises at all times. (This may help you meet fire regulations too.) Don't let strangers and contractors wander around the site.

Call in the crime prevention officer from your local police. They can provide straightforward advice, and keeping in contact with them may give you 'heads-up' warnings should there be potential local problems occurring. If you can, fit an alarm, and make sure it's well monitored. The police will sometimes put people and companies on a 'non-attendance' list if their alarms keep firing off false alerts.

Lock valuable stuff – laptops, server devices, etc. – away. Don't display your equipment in open view. If you get a delivery of new equipment, don't leave the empty boxes on the street on bin day. Someone will notice you've got some new kit.

## education is vital

Educating your staff is perhaps the most cost-effective control you can implement, since most security incidents are attributable to human error or misunderstanding. Make sure everyone is aware of the basic security threats to your business. They also need to know what their own specific responsibilities are, and what's expected of them.

Make sure staff know what a virus is, what it looks like, how to deal with one, and who to report it to when it happens. If there are other specific threats you have concerns about, ensure staff know the relevant what, how and who?

## access control

If your IT has an ID and password facility, use it. Make sure everyone has their own ID, and that they know not to divulge it to anyone else. Do not give people more facilities than they need to do their job. If you can, make sure that usage of computer systems is logged. (Most systems provide this automatically.)

## keeping desks clear

Clear your desk at the end of each day, and ask your staff to do the same. They don't have to lock their working papers away. Putting them into a desk drawer provides significant protection against casual theft, as well as fire and flood. This is another low-cost, high-value control.

## destruction

Get rid of sensitive information carefully. If it is very sensitive, get a shredder. If the quantity of information is too great for this, many companies provide mobile/ specialist destruction services, and provide 'certificates of destruction' for masses of paper and other media, including CDs.

## CHECKLIST

- ☐ backup your system – not just your data

- ☐ change all vendor-supplied passwords on user and administrator accounts immediately before you use them

- ☐ check your system event logs now and then for anything suspicious

- ☐ clear out all temporary files and temporary Internet cache files periodically. Your office systems have a simple wizard program that can take you through this process

- ☐ periodically check to see if all user IDs on the system are needed. If the original owners have moved on, suspend the relevant user accounts. Check to see if there's anything of importance stored under these accounts. If there isn't and after three months no one has complained about the suspension you should be safe to delete it

- ☐ every so often remind all your people of their security responsibilities

- ☐ go to your relevant office software update sites – Microsoft Windows, Office, etc – and apply all updates. Remember that some of these involve big files (eg. Windows XP service packs). It may prove sensible to download the file once and burn it to CD and use this to update all machines. Your choice will depend on your connection speed

- ☐ keep all your technical documentation, key holders' names/addresses, etc. up to date

- ☐ keep your equipment tidy and clean. Most unwanted events are due to simple things like loose wires and build ups of dust

- ☐ make a list of all your equipment and keep it up to date. Keep a copy of this list off-site. It may prove invaluable in an insurance claim

- ☐ make sure all door/window keys are accounted for, and that burglar alarm codes are changed on a regular basis

- ☐ make sure all system clocks are set to the same time. Many systems do this automatically – check with your supplier

- ☐ make sure all your security kit, processes and procedures are working as expected – test them. For example, check that the pictures from your CCTV (should you use it) are of suitable quality

- ☐ make sure you don't run out of disk space. Keep a close eye on capacity status. You can crash lots of programs by having no disk space left

- ☐ take a backup of your system and test it

- ☐ move backup tapes away from your primary site, and replace your backup media periodically

- ☐ update all your anti-virus software and make sure it's current on all devices, including servers, desktops and laptops. Make sure you get regular updates from your vendor across the Internet

# risk management

How do you balance the cost of minimising potential threats with maximising your investments and opportunities? Ted Humphreys, information security consultant at XiSEC, explains

What are information security risks? And, why should businesses be concerned about them? In simple terms the risks we are concerned about are information security incidents or breaches that could result in an unfavourable impact on the business: not being able to survive in competitive markets, making losses not profits, damage to image and reputation, or lack of growth in the business or decline in the overall wellbeing of the business.

The first thing a company needs to do is to identify what could go wrong to cause an incident or breach and how likely it is. Next, it needs to determine how severe the damage could be and decide what action it should take to protect itself against such incidents and breaches to limit any undesirable impact.

## EXECUTIVE SUMMARY

☐ risk management is a continual process that addresses new emerging risks

☐ it's better to know what you're up against and prepare accordingly

☐ ISO/IEC 17799 recommends a wide range of best practice measures that are effective, but not expensive

## what should we be protecting?

Of prime concern is information that is essential, sensitive and/or critical to the wellbeing, profitability, growth and stability of the company. You need to ask:

☐ could it be leaked to a competitor?

☐ is it vulnerable to being corrupted, damaged or lost?

☐ is it available to authorised access when it is needed?

All these issues can be addressed by considering risks.

Depending on what form the information is in, this may include protecting how it is stored, processed and communicated. Depending on where it is kept and how it is used and processed, information can be subject to many different kinds of threat. Is it in paper form, in electronic form in computer systems, being sent across the Internet, presented verbally between business partners or work colleagues, stored on CD/DVD media or on a mobile device?

## what are we protecting against?

Today's business environment is subject to many types of threat. These threats may never cause you any harm but, nevertheless, they will continue to exist and are likely to grow in number, as new types of threats are generated every day. (See also Chapter 2 for more on computer threats, and Chapter 9 on employee-related problems).

A clear example is the PC connected to the Internet – if it has no protection to detect and destroy viruses then this is a weakness open for exploitation. Files, documents and information on the PC could be destroyed by a virus. This is a well-known problem for which there is a tried-and-tested solution: installation of anti-virus software which is easy to install and use. There are many other examples of vulnerabilities where the solution is not as straightforward, and this is where risk management can help.

The DTI's Information Security Breaches Survey 2004, which is carried out every two years, provides a snapshot of a growing trend in the incidents that businesses are faced with. Examples given in the survey include:

- ☐ virus infection and disruptive software
- ☐ staff misuse of information systems
- ☐ system failures
- ☐ data corruption
- ☐ unauthorised access by outsiders, including competitors and hackers
- ☐ unsolicited emails (spam)
- ☐ denial of service attacks

- ☐ disgruntled employees
- ☐ fraud, theft and deception

These incidents may be caused through threats exploiting a variety of weaknesses within the company and the systems and processes it uses. For example:

- ☐ lack of effective company policy and procedures for handling information and using company facilities
- ☐ lack of user training and awareness
- ☐ weak access control on IT systems
- ☐ no allocation of responsibilities
- ☐ no system planning
- ☐ lack of maintenance
- ☐ no information back-up

## risk and cost assessment

So, it's better to be prepared by knowing the risks your company faces and to do something to control them rather than suffer serious consequences and impacts through lack of knowledge and motivation to take action. A company therefore needs to assess what its risks are, by:

- ☐ identifying how likely it is that threats and incidents, such as those quoted above might occur, taking into account its own specific environment
- ☐ estimating how exposed the company is in terms of impact, loss or damage, given the likelihood that the incident or breach might occur

The cost of any action taken to control the risks should be proportionate to the severity of the impact and business benefits gained:

- ☐ what are the direct financial losses (revenues, profit, market share)?
- ☐ what is the cost of replacing or repairing lost or damaged assets (re-establishing a corrupted customer database, theft of equipment, etc.)?
- ☐ what is the cost of implementing information security?

The balance is the cost of minimising the risks against maximising business investments and opportunities.

## managing the risks

The cost of information security does not need to be high. There are many best practice controls from the ISO/IEC 17799 international standard (previously known as BS 7799 Part 1) that do not involve the purchase, installation and maintenance of technology but nevertheless they provide effective protection against many types of threat.

ISO/IEC 17799 covers a wide range of best practice for managing risks across different areas of the business, including organisational, human resources, third-party services, business operations and communications and legal and regulatory compliance. It has become the 'common language' in the international business community that is used to protect against the continuing threats to information systems. These controls always need to be supplemented with additional management best practice to keep the standard up to date. The next edition of ISO/IEC 17799 will be published in June-July 2005.

## keeping up to date

Finally, having assessed the risks and implemented a suitable set of controls to manage them, a company should review the situation on a regular basis in line with changes to the business environment. The company might introduce new systems or working practices, the workforce might change, new lines of business might be adopted and new threats might be identified.

To ensure the investment in information security is maintained, it is important that the company monitors and reviews its risks on a regular basis, and that it makes improvements to its protection.

# employees: the weakest link

Employees can cause untold damage to a business, deliberately or unintentionally. Ted Humphreys, information security consultant at XiSEC, advises on how to get your workforce onside

## EXECUTIVE SUMMARY

☐ a security policy must be enforced at all levels within the business if it is to be effective

☐ employee awareness is key to successful implementation of information security

☐ employees must recognise that they're all required to deploy security practices, in one form or another

Protecting your company requires a workforce that is:

☐    aware of the risks

☐    aware of their responsibilities to act in a sensible and secure way

☐    applying the policies and best practice adopted by the business

☐    responsive to the reporting of security incidents

☐    mindful of their legal responsibilities

This requires action from both management, which needs to put in place a framework to create and implement security policy, best practice and awareness, and from employees, who must work within this management framework.

## breaches of security

There is ongoing evidence that in many cases breaches of information security are caused by or with the involvement of employees. The DTI's Information

Security Breaches Survey 2004 states: "Human error rather than flawed technology is the root cause of most security breaches. So, the challenge for many organisations is to create a security-aware culture."

Breaches may be caused accidentally – due to a lack of understanding, training or awareness – or through human errors or mistakes. On the other hand, they may be caused by a deliberate attempt to breach security for personal gain, to defraud the business, or by a disgruntled employee causing malicious damage to the business's facilities.

Implementing effective information security is, therefore, highly critical and dependent on employees' participation and commitment to help safeguard the assets of the company.

## collective responsibility

No matter what the job entails, all employees need to implement some information security best practice in their day-to-day work. How much security will depend on the specific job function the individual is employed to do. Employers need to assess the level of risk posed by each employee by asking, for example:

- [ ] does the employee handle personal data?

- [ ] does the job involve company confidential information?

- [ ] does the work involve maintaining IT systems or just using such systems?

- [ ] is the employee engaged in business activities that require using computing off-site, in meetings or at clients' sites?

These and many other job activities require employees to apply information security.

## before, during and after employment

The international standard ISO/IEC 17799 (previously known as BS 7799 Part 1) is a Code of Practice for Information Security. This provides a broad range of best practice for information security that can be used as a management framework.

The standard deals with what needs to be considered and done regarding:

- before employment (what action management and those dealing with human resources need to consider during the recruitment stage):
  - processing applications, interviews, job descriptions
  - background checks, verification of qualifications
  - contracts, terms and conditions of employment, confidentiality agreements
- during employment (this considers security in the day-to-day job functions of the employee):
  - relevant training and awareness
  - use of procedures
  - allocation and review of appropriate access rights, privileges and responsibilities
  - taking regular back-ups
  - reporting security incidents such as viruses, unusual behaviour, etc.
  - processing company information of varying levels of sensitivity
- after employment (what action management and the human resources group need to take during termination of employment):
  - contract closure, confidentiality agreements and completion of paperwork for termination employment
  - return of equipment
  - removal of access rights

## awareness and training

Effective employee awareness is key to successful implementation of information security. This can be achieved by providing:

- staff handbooks and manuals
- contracts and letters of employment

- ☐ induction exercises after joining the company, or on transferring to another job function within the company

- ☐ training courses and ongoing on-the-job training

- ☐ specific work instructions or procedures

## keeping it relevant

Whatever methods are used, all employees should receive some sort of security awareness training that is relevant and appropriate to their job function, role and responsibilities within the company. Security awareness should include information on known threats and risks, who to contact for further security advice and the proper channels for reporting incidents.

There are some job functions that will require employees to carry out more specific security activities. For example, someone dealing with the IT for the company is typically responsible for the testing, installation and configuration of software and computer systems and this will need more specific security awareness and training. There should be someone in the company who is responsible for physical security and someone who deals with personal data, for example, working in the human resources department.

## social engineering

Employers need to be aware of the dangers resulting from social engineering, ie. the practice of outsiders getting employees to do things that they might not otherwise want to. This includes preying on people's fears, trust, their need to please, or their lack of awareness. It is a powerful way of exploiting vulnerabilities in an organisation.

There are many examples of social engineering leading to breaches of security. One is the highly authentic looking email that appears to be from your bank, that claims your online account has been compromised and asks you to log in and change your password at once. However, an incident of this nature can just as easily happen over the telephone, with a caller presenting a perfectly realistic scenario, designed to get you to divulge sensitive or personal information.

---

## A DOSE OF BEST PRACTICE

Make sure your employees are aware of what to do with regard to:

- ☐ backups
- ☐ viruses and other types of malicious software
- ☐ misuse of company resources
- ☐ Internet and email scams
- ☐ proper use of the Internet
- ☐ handling of sensitive and personal data
- ☐ abiding by the law

---

Employees should be aware, suspicious and mindful, of:

- ☐ emails that appear to be official and linked to your bank, credit card supplier or other organisations you normally deal with. If you are suspicious retype the usual URL you have for these organisations rather than relying on what is in the email. Be aware of other information contained in such emails and always go to the real website and get the official contact details

- ☐ eye-catching email titles that are designed to lure the recipient into opening emails and possibly downloading undesirable files

- ☐ requests for your password or PIN numbers over the phone or via email. Some of these requests might be genuine

- ☐ callers asking for sensitive information. If necessary, take the caller's name and telephone number and tell them that you will call them back. If such requests are legitimate then employees have done no harm by being cautious. If it's a scam, they have helped to protect the business and themselves by taking appropriate action

## reporting incidents and problems

All employees should be made aware of their responsibility to report any information security incidents and problems as quickly as possible. They should be given training in using procedures for reporting information security incidents.

Employees should know who to report incidents to and understand the need to report such incidents in a timely manner.

The types of incidents that should be considered include:

☐ unusual system behaviour – especially when connected to the Internet caused – eg. by viruses, worms and other types malicious software codes or spam

☐ spyware, adware and other invasive activities

☐ system malfunctions (eg. software and/or hardware), system crashes, overloads or degradation in system performance

☐ breaches of physical security, including unauthorised access or damage to, or theft of physical property and equipment

☐ breaches of confidentiality

☐ suspicious callers, telephone requests and email scams

## legal responsibilities

Employees should be made aware of their legal responsibilities. There are various UK laws and regulations that apply to many aspects of an employee's day-to-day work such as the handling of personal data, use of the Internet and email, unauthorised access into other people's systems, copyright and software licences, fraud, theft and damage to other people's property. In addition, online trading brings businesses into the realms of foreign and international laws.

An employee may accidentally or deliberately cause damage by introducing a virus into someone's system, or they may try and attempt to gain access to another organisation's system, or even to send libellous emails. It is important that employees understand which laws and regulations apply to them, that they are given clear guidance and procedures from management of working within these laws and that they know their employee rights and responsibilities.

Management can manage employee risks more effectively by providing awareness of the relevant legislation. (See chapter 10 for more on this.)

# what the law says

**What liabilities does a company have if it fails to adopt
robust system security measures? Shelagh Gaskill, head
of the Information Law practice at Pinsent Masons,
highlights potential areas of culpability**

In today's highly regulated environment, companies have their work cut out for them as they struggle to implement ever-increasing volumes of legislation and to comply with corporate governance rules. In addition, they must also keep up with the many advances in technology, while battling the growing threat from those who would use technology against them. Next generation computer viruses, surveillance methods and sophisticated interception tools render systems more vulnerable to external and internal attack. Ensuring that a company is up to date with its system security measures is now a fundamental part of its security strategy.

## EXECUTIVE SUMMARY

☐ the Data Protection Act 1998 affects any company that handles, processes or holds personal data

☐ failure to comply with legal or regulatory obligations can lead to a damaged reputation

☐ even worse than being bombarded by spam is discovering that you are the unwitting sender

☐ establishing audit trails and monitoring data traffic and online activities is critical

Any business that fails to implement and maintain appropriate and up-to-date system security measures is exposing itself to legal and regulatory attacks from supervisory authorities and affected third parties. There are several ways in which a breach of systems security may give rise to corporate liability.

These include liability:

☐ under the Data Protection Act 1998

☐ for disclosing confidential information in breach of a contract or licence term

- ☐ for the unauthorised access and use of a third party's intellectual property rights

- ☐ under the Company (Audit Investigations and Community Enterprise) Act 2004

- ☐ under the Regulation of Investigatory Powers Act 2000

Each of these areas is described in more detail below.

# Data Protection Act 1998

Virtually every company processes personal data about individuals to some degree. This information is not just essential to the running of a company (eg. employee or business contact data), but may also be one of a company's most valuable assets (eg. customer databases or marketing lists). The Data Protection Act 1998 requires companies to take appropriate technical and organisational measures to safeguard personal data against unauthorised or unlawful processing, accidental loss, destruction or damage. For example, if someone hacks into a company's computer system and downloads data relating to its customers or employees, the company is liable for that breach if its security measures are found to be inappropriate to safeguard against such attack.

Failure to comply with the requirements of the Act may result in enforcement action from the Information Commissioner, legal action from any affected individual and, in certain circumstances, could ultimately expose directors and other officers of a company to personal criminal liability. Clearly, the negative publicity surrounding enforcement or legal action is unlikely to benefit anyone.

On the positive side, the Act does not require a company to adopt state-of-the-art security measures or incur excessive cost. However, it does require companies to adopt security measures that are appropriate to the harm that might result from a breach, taking into account the nature of the data being protected. The more sensitive the data, eg. medical information, the greater the harm that can be caused to an individual in the event of a security breach. Therefore, the measures taken must be sufficient to safeguard against such harm. Some security measures are fairly standard, such as virus detecting software and encryption tools. However, simply having these measures is not enough if they are not kept up to date.

Where a company detects that its computer system has been accessed without its authority, it will need to ascertain what damage, if any, has been caused. This damage could take the form of data being added, altered, deleted or downloaded from databases. In some cases companies have been inundated with spam, while in others they've discovered, to their horror, that they are the ones sending the spam. The cost of detecting such interference can be significant since such activity is not always immediately obvious without careful investigation. Nevertheless, companies have an obligation to ensure that any personal data that they hold is, and remains, accurate. They must, therefore, have appropriate mechanisms in place to enable them to check whether accuracy has been compromised. One of the ways in which a company can track access and use of its systems is by using audit trails. This is particularly important for those companies who trade data as a commercial asset. For example, a list broker may be asked to warrant the accuracy of its marketing lists and must, therefore, have a way of ensuring the integrity of its data so that it can give that warranty with certainty.

Where a company is acting as a data processor (ie. it is processing data on behalf of another company), then a breach of its computer systems may expose it to liability under its processing contract. Examples of data processors might include companies providing outsourced services, such as payroll, recruitment or IT.

## confidentiality

It is usual to find confidentiality provisions in most contracts. These typically prohibit the disclosure of any information that the disclosing party considers to be confidential to its business. Where the recipient company stores such confidential information on its computer systems, it must take all reasonable and appropriate security measures to safeguard that information from unauthorised access. A breach of systems security that causes the disclosure of confidential information is likely to result in a breach of contract. Furthermore, if the recipient company acted negligently in not having appropriate security measures in place, or ignoring any potential risks, then its directors could also be held to be responsible if they were found to have acted negligently.

## intellectual property rights

A third party may license its intellectual property rights to a company. These rights are typically restricted in scope, and their use and disclosure to anyone other than the licensee and its authorised users will usually be prohibited. Where the licensee holds this intellectual property on its systems it will need to ensure it has appropriate and reasonable security measures in place to restrict any disclosures to unauthorised parties, or to prevent unauthorised parties from gaining access to the intellectual property. Clearly, any failure to do so can result in a breach of contract or licence. This can have a significant impact on a company if the consequence is the breach of a software licence or know-how licence resulting in its termination.

## Company (Audit Investigations and Community Enterprise) Act 2004

This Act, which is the UK equivalent of the US Sarbanes Oxley Act, reinforces the existing duties on companies and officers to furnish auditors (both in the UK and parent company auditors based abroad) and, in certain circumstances the government, with information, and makes it a criminal offence to provide misleading or false information. Similar sanctions are imposed for false or misleading statements made in directors' reports, and there is a general duty to have full and accurate information available when required. None of these requirements can be achieved satisfactorily from systems with inadequate security.

## Regulation of Investigatory Powers Act 2000

In order to ensure that systems are secure, it is necessary to establish audit trails and to monitor traffic data and online activities. The Lawful Business Practice Regulations made under the Act (RIPA Regulations for short) give businesses plenty of grounds for monitoring so long as the communications they monitor are business communications.

If a business allows its employees reasonable private use of business equipment, this causes a problem for monitoring because the RIPA Regulations will not apply and the only grounds for monitoring is the consent of both parties. It is very easy to get consent from employees. This is usually done by inserting a paragraph in the company's communications policy. However, it is very difficult to get consent from the people outside the company with whom the employees communicate. The method used by most City law firms is to add an explanation at the end of email messages stating that by communicating with their employees by email after having read the explanation, they will be deemed to have consented to having their communications monitored if serious breaches of the communications policy are suspected.

## PRACTICAL STEPS

There are a number of practical steps that a company can take to maintain systems security. These include:

- [ ] implementing a security policy for employees and third parties using company computer systems. The policy should cover areas such as access control to systems, virus protection, email and Internet use and compliance with the requirements of the Data Protection Act 1998

- [ ] implementing appropriate technical and organisational measures to back up the requirements of the security policy. Examples of technical measures include anti-virus and anti-spam software, encryption tools, audit trails and firewalls. These all need to be kept up-to-date to be effective. Examples of organisational measures include having a clear desk policy, locking offices and desks when not in use, positioning computer monitors away from public areas and changing passwords frequently

- [ ] ensuring clear accountabilities and responsibilities for security, with clear management accountability, incident management, and reporting and handling of issues

- [ ] ensuring that employees are trained on security requirements, including the care and handling of personal data, so that they're aware of their obligations and the risks of non-compliance

# getting help

Security is a topic you want to be sure to get the best advice on, says Marc Beishon, business and technology writer

As security has taken hold as a major issue for companies, the number of sources offering advice and help has increased greatly. Both from a strategic viewpoint and for day-to-day implementation, it's important not to overlook such access to support. In this chapter we describe the main categories of advice, support and supply. (See the resources section for website addresses of the organisations mentioned.)

## government

The government has a vested interest in security from several standpoints, in particular, the fight against 'cyber crime', the stability of electronic commerce (especially since a good deal of its business is now conducted online) and in contributing sound advice to companies.

### EXECUTIVE SUMMARY

- [ ] the DTI is a primary source of help for SMEs grappling with IT and communications security
- [ ] special interest online groups can guide you on new problems
- [ ] law firms are another source of useful information

As the sponsor of this guide, the Department of Trade and Industry (DTI) is a primary source of guidance on security for communications and IT systems, particularly those used by small and medium-sized companies. The DTI has recently consolidated its guidance on the Best Practice section of its website – there is a dedicated section for security with a comprehensive list of short business guides that can be downloaded. The topics include guides on standards, viruses, inappropriate usage and unauthorised access, systems failure and theft. There is also an online security healthcheck, and a facility to 'ask an expert' by email.

Other government initiatives include:

- Businesslink, which provides advice on selecting IT suppliers and also has information on security topics such as data protection

- ITsafe – a service designed to provide home users and small businesses with plain English advice to help protect computers, mobile phones and other devices from malicious attack

- the Information Commissioner's Office, which oversees the Data Protection Act and other regulations such as the Privacy and Electronic Communications rules

- the Central Sponsor for Information Assurance – a Cabinet Office unit that promotes a 'culture of security' for the public and private sectors

- the National Hi-Tech Crime Unit, which is mainly concerned with Internet crime and has published a report on threats to businesses

- the National Infrastructure Security Co-ordination Centre, which is responsible for threat assessment of major attacks on IT systems and promoting best practice

- the Information Assurance and Certification Services (IACS), which is run by Communications-Electronics Security Group, the information assurance arm of GCHQ. It provides services and advice mainly to public and private infrastructure organisations. Its website has a list of companies that provide security audits and other services

## online resources

There is a plethora of websites dedicated to security, but most focus on technical information about specific threats and vulnerabilities in computer operating systems. Security Focus is one such example. Nonetheless, there are often also useful columns commenting on latest trends such as 'phishing'.

Indeed, there are also special interest groups springing up to promote solutions to emerging problems, such as the Anti-Phishing Working Group. There are also technology groups, such as the Wi-Fi Alliance, that have information about the latest security certification standards for vendors' equipment.

One US site with an obvious security focus is the Internet Security Alliance. In 2004 it brought out the *Common Sense Guide to Cyber Security for Small Businesses*, which can be downloaded and includes a comprehensive set of 'practice tips' that may prove useful.

Another particularly useful site is that of the SANS (SysAdmin, Audit, Network, Security) Institute. Although it is mostly technical, it does have a resource section where it reproduces best practice policy templates developed by large organisations. You can download policies such as:

- [ ] acceptable use of using computers/Internet
- [ ] anti-virus guidelines
- [ ] email content and retention
- [ ] remote dial-in
- [ ] information sensitivity

In all, there are 24 policy templates and they provide a good idea of the scope of issues a policy needs to cover in a large organisation. However, certain policies – such as acceptable use and anti-virus – apply to all. See 'sample policies' on the website.

## agencies, consultants and analysts

The British Standards Institute is clearly the first port of call for information on the British standard for information security (BS 7799). The site of the Information Security Management Systems (ISMS) User Group is dedicated to information about BS 7799, and has an excellent 'FAQ' section.

One of the leading agencies is the Information Assurance Advisory Council, which takes a business-oriented approach to best practice in information security. Its website includes a series of best practice guidelines aimed at directors.

One consultancy specialising in these top-level issues is IT Governance, which has copious board-level material on its site. The founder is author of *IT Governance: a Manager's Guide to Data Security and BS 7799/ISO 17799*, published by Kogan Page.

Most of the major consultancy and analysts firms have some form of security expertise and there are some that specialise in the topic. Major analysts such as Gartner, Ovum and Forrester are primary sources of information and research, and the consulting arms of the big accountancy firms are also strong across most IT advice. In particular, PricewaterhouseCoopers, in conjunction with the DTI, has managed the last two Information Security Breaches Surveys. There is a dedicated website that comprises the survey results, and fact sheets on the major problems such as intrusion prevention, viruses, spam and remote access.

The National Computing Centre runs basic vulnerability tests and provides information and research across the IT spectrum.

Consultancies that specialise in security include:

- ☐ Sec-Tec, whose services include penetration testing and security awareness training

- ☐ Corsaire, which is an all round security consultancy

- ☐ Computer Crime Consultants, which offers services in IT security and computer crime detection, investigation, prosecution and prevention

- ☐ Insight Consulting, which is an all-round player focusing on information security, business continuity and risk management.

## law firms

Legal issues affect a company's security in many ways – from data protection, to email libel, to ecommerce transactions. So, it is not surprising that several law firms have established technology practices that major on these issues. Apart from being obvious sources of counsel, you can also find information on their websites.

## primary vendors

There is now an extraordinary number of players engaged either directly or indirectly in the IT security market. These range from major global players with large product sets to niche vendors of technology such as the latest email or spam filtering tools.

They include vendors of:

- ☐ anti-virus and firewalls
- ☐ intrusion detection systems
- ☐ password/authentication systems
- ☐ network security solutions, fixed and wireless
- ☐ telephony and converged voice/data systems
- ☐ ecommerce system providers
- ☐ anti-spam/email solutions
- ☐ remote access/virtual private network
- ☐ website security

Vendors have a keen interest in educating the market about security. Many have produced white papers on a wide spectrum of issues, although some are pitched at expert level and comprise heavyweight technical detail. Some, especially the large anti-virus players such as McAfee and Symantec, have produced UK business guides to security that are well worth sourcing. Microsoft is also a good port of call. Its UK business security guide is a worthy response to the frequent criticism it's received for weaknesses in its ubiquitous operating environment.

The best vendors also run excellent programmes for their resellers. This will certainly show in the quality of the materials and advice you can obtain from the firms charged with direct selling to businesses.

As a gauge to the imagination that some vendors are applying to products, see Pointsec's PicturePIN access control, which consists of a series of pictures chosen by the user from a randomly displayed, larger gallery. Instead of having to remember a password the user simply points out the pictures corresponding to a 'story' only they know.

## resellers and integrators

For many companies, especially SMEs, a first point of contact for IT issues is the supplier of their systems. These firms are usually resellers and integrators of products supplied by large vendors. Security should be a priority for all companies installing IT systems, but clearly some have more expertise than others. It pays to assess potential partners carefully, especially where technologies such as wireless and mobile systems are being deployed. Companies likely to be strong in security issues include those that specialise in networks.

A good way of tracking down security expertise is to visit the sites of distributors that specialise in security, such as Global Secure Solutions and e92plus.

General guidance and pointers to best practice in IT procurement can be found on the BusinessLink, DTI and BuyIT sites.

## service providers

Given that many applications can be hosted remotely over the Internet, it's not surprising that suppliers are setting up 'managed services' to monitor or host certain applications, including security. There are several types to note:

- [ ] firms that remotely scan and probe for security weaknesses (such as out-of-date operating software) and for the presence of unauthorised software
- [ ] email filtering services – checking for viruses and spam
- [ ] providers of private networks and firewall services
- [ ] firms that host ecommerce and other critical applications
- [ ] online backup services

BT, for example, is a major supplier in this market. In general, signing up to an 'outsourced' service provider can give round-the-clock access to certified security expertise that is rarely available inhouse.

## events

There are several dedicated exhibitions with associated conference sessions in the UK. If you're unable to attend them, their websites are useful for sourcing news and contacts for vendors and service providers. The Infosecurity show is one of the largest. Others include IIPSEC and Intersec, the last of which concentrates mostly on major crime. Other exhibitions on Internet and wireless technologies are also good sources of information and contacts.

# the next five years

In the future, businesses will face the paradox of secure openness, which will mean reconciling the need for fast and free exchange of information, with that of protecting their intellectual assets, says Professor Jim Norton, senior policy adviser on ebusiness, IoD

At the heart of all successful business is the creative management of risk – no risk, no profit. There are few genuinely new risks, but the increasing use of new technologies offers great scope for 'old' risks – such as disaffected staff – to offer new challenges.

The last five years have seen the Internet and the tools of ebusiness, such as networked information systems, being taken up by mainstream enterprises of all sizes. Increasingly, they are an essential element of business life and, as such, present further risks to be managed.

It seems inevitable that global economic trends, including the continued international outsourcing both of lower value manufac-

**EXECUTIVE SUMMARY**

☐ increasing competition will intensify business's security needs

☐ increased reliance on quick access to information will be seen across all sectors and sizes of business

☐ mobile and wireless technologies will bring further security risks

☐ combating denial of service attacks will be the biggest challenge

turing and 'back office' services, will place further reliance on the secure creation, storage and exchange of information. Therefore, a holistic and rigorous approach to information security will be a key determinant for sustainable business success.

## key developments

For better or worse, six key trends are likely to shape developments over the next five years. Three represent key business or regulatory drivers and three new technological capabilities.

## capturing tacit and explicit knowledge

For developed economies, their continuing competitive advantage will be based on the extent to which their companies can capture, and more rapidly exploit, the knowledge developed from their operations. The way in which such companies can give key staff a real incentive to codify their explicit knowledge into 'knowledge management' systems, and to share their tacit knowledge securely with colleagues in physical clusters and innovation centres, will be vital for success.

## squeezing out the slack

Continuously intensifying competition, across all sectors, will lead to ever leaner (and meaner) business models. The excessive cost of carrying stock or staff beyond a bare minimum will lead to very tightly coupled supply chain models. Such models are exceptionally intolerant of any disruption.

## increasing transparency

There will be growing demand for quoted companies to report to shareholders and markets in greater depth and with increasing frequency. The Operating Financial Review is perhaps only the tip of a deeply worrying iceberg. The need for high levels of transparency and verifiability will place exceptional demands on corporate information systems.

## increasing mobility

Within the company, systems will increasingly be linked wirelessly to enable 'hot desking' and rapid re-configuration. Outside the office, staff will increasingly demand the same ease of access to key data and systems from a 'virtual' desktop, whether they are on the move or at a customer's premises.

## IP rules OK?

The convergence of all networking – both fixed and mobile – around IP (Internet Protocol) has had many false starts. However, it is now leading to the genuine convergence of voice and data communications. Use of Voice over IP (VoIP) services will grow dramatically, offering further security challenges.

### third-party dependencies

Many companies will outsource key parts of their information systems to third-party providers. 'Grid computing' will start to make an impact with early adopters testing large-scale rental models for applications, processing and storage. The security implications of such a 'mixed economy' are not always well understood.

## likely impacts

All of these developments lead to business models that contain an implicit paradox. Information becomes the corporate lifeblood. It has to be shared on a highly targeted, but increasingly extensive, basis with key contacts inside the business and in partnerships up and down supply chains.

And yet, disruption to these information flows, and loss, falsification or misappropriation of key information, could have devastating effects. Simple and easy authorised access anywhere, anytime is desired. But, meanwhile, businesses have to build exceptional defences against unauthorised access and use.

The challenge for information security professionals for at least the next five years is to resolve this paradox of 'secure openness'. Key issues will include:

### winning hearts and minds

Successful security systems work with, rather than against, staff. It is vital to communicate why such systems are necessary and to demonstrate that users' needs have been taken into account as fully as possible. The best technology can often be undermined by poor attention to this 'people aspect' of design.

### designing in integrity

Businesses must avoid dependencies on single individuals or single technologies. We are used to the idea, for example, of a safe with two separate locks that can be operated simultaneously by different individuals. Such a 'dual key' approach, requiring separate individuals to act together, is at the heart of good electronic security design. Similarly, using a range of different technologies to provide in-depth electronic security is a sensible investment.

### redundancy rather than backups

New technologies that exploit the wide availability of optical fibre communications enable the mirroring of data in real-time on widely separated sites. In the event that the primary site is lost, processing can continue from an alternative site straight away. And, there's no need to multiply data volumes by making offsite backups.

### good identity management

The first step in security is to be able to identify unambiguously the authorised users. This increasingly requires three elements: something a person 'is' – for example a biometric test such as fingerprint or retina scan, something he or she 'has' – such as a smartcard with an embedded secure key, and something he or she 'knows' – such as a personal password. However, the surrounding personnel processes must also be good. Great care is required in verifying an individual's identity when they join the company. Equally important is the immediate removal and revocation of access when they leave.

### protecting against 'denial of service'

Perhaps the biggest challenge over the next five years will be combating the cyber equivalent of a sit down protest outside a retail store. This is known as the 'distributed denial of service' (DDoS) attack. Networks of thousands (or even hundreds of thousands) of PCs that are not properly protected against virus infections can be co-opted in attacks on companies, flooding websites or portals with false traffic. Filtering out this traffic before it can jam an organisation's access connections requires a high degree of collaboration with the information service provider or telecommunications operator that supports the company's systems.

## final thoughts

Managing authorised access to critical information both inside and outside the enterprise will be a continuing challenge. As information increasingly represents the oxygen of corporate life, businesses need to avoid suffocation – where information is not shared in a timely way – while at the same time preventing that oxygen from leaking away to others.

Anti-Phishing Working Group
www.antiphishing.org

British Standards Institute
www.bsi-global.com

Business Continuity Institute
www.thebci.org

Businesslink
www.businesslink.gov.uk

BuyIT
www.buyitnet.org

Central Sponsor for Information Assurance
www.cabinetoffice.gov.uk/csia

Computer Crime Consultants
www.ccc-ltd.com

CERT Coordination Center
www.cert.org

Computer Security Resource Center
http://csrc.nist.gov

Corsaire
www.corsaire.com

Department of Trade and Industry – business advice pages
www.dti.gov.uk/bestpractice/infosec

Department of Trade and Industry – security section
www.dti.gov.uk/industries/information_security

e92plus
www.92plus.com

Global Secure Solutions www.gsec.co.uk

Home Computing Initiatives
www.ukhomecomputing.co.uk

Information Assurance Advisory Council
www.iaac.org.uk

Information Assurance and Certification Services (IACS)
www.cesg.gov.uk

Information Commissioner's Office
www.informationcommissioner.gov.uk

Information Security Breaches Survey 2004 (DTI/PricewaterhouseCoopers)
www.security-survey.gov.uk

Information security healthcheck
www.dti-bestpractice-tools.org/healthcheck

Information Warfare Site
www.iwar.org.uk/comsec

Infosecurity Europe (annual security event)
www.infosec.co.uk

Insight Consulting
www.insight.co.uk

Internet Security Alliance
www.isalliance.org

Internet Watch Foundation
www.iwf.org.uk

ISMS International User Group
www.xisec.com

ITsafe
www.itsafe.gov.uk

ITsecurity.com: the Encyclopedia of Computer Security
www.itsecurity.com

IT Governance (founder is author of *IT Governance: A Manager's Guide to Data Security and BS 7799/ISO 17799*, Kogan Page)
www.itgovernance.co.uk

Microsoft
www.microsoft.com/security

National Computing Centre
www.ncc.co.uk

National Hi-Tech Crime Unit
www.nhtcu.org

National Infrastructure Security Co-ordination Centre
www.niscc.gov.uk

Open Web Application Security Project
www.owasp.org

PricewaterhouseCoopers
www.pwc.com/security

Pointsec
www.pointsec.com

SANS (SysAdmin, Audit, Network, Security) Institute –
www.sans.org

Sec-Tec
www.sec-tec.com

Security Focus
www.securityfocus.com

Unified Incident Reporting and Alert Scheme (UNIRAS)
www.uniras.gov.uk

Virus hoaxes
http://vil.mcafee.com/hoax.asp

VNUnet
www.vnunet.com/security

Whitehats Network Security Resource
www.whitehats.com

Wi-Fi Alliance
www.wi-fi.org

## the security health benchmark

The DTI has developed a security healthcheck tool that is available at www.dti-bestpractice-tools.org/healthcheck to help SMEs and similar organisations measure their security health.

The healthcheck provides an initial series of simple questions that will help give an indication of where your organisation stands regarding BS 7799, the UK standard for managing Information Security. The questions included in the healthcheck are:

1. does your organisation have an information security policy?

2. are staff allocated with specific security responsibilities, eg. locking the building, allocating passwords?

3. do you know what your organisation's main assets are, do you have a list of them, and does this list include information?

4. are specific personnel measures, such as training users or including security in their job descriptions, taken with respect to security?

5. does your organisation take steps to prevent unauthorised access to your premises?

6. have you implemented operational controls and procedures to safeguard your information, eg. use of backups, anti virus software, firewalls?

7. do you control access to information through the effective use of user IDs and passwords, eg. making sure users don't share passwords, write their passwords on Post-it notes?

8. have steps been taken to ensure that security requirements are defined and incorporated during system development or met by packaged software solutions?

9. do you have any business continuity plans?

10. do you ensure that you meet all your legal requirements/obligations, eg. licensing, copyright, data protection?

If you are familiar with BS 7799, you will recognise the questions as matching the headings within the standard. The tool can take you into greater detail if you want.

You can use the online tool directly or ask yourself each question offline, taking on board the comments below, listed under each section.

### Does your organisation have an information security policy?

No policy ever directly made anything more secure. However, a rational, well-written set of policies covering the main areas of interest to security can pay dividends. For example, providing clear direction on the way information is handled makes errors less likely to occur, and also provides a means by which employers can take malevolent employees to court should they misuse systems.

### Are staff allocated with specific security responsibilities, eg. locking the building, allocating passwords?

If people know what to do, and understand their responsibilities, they are much less likely to cause errors. They are also more likely to report unwanted events, and thereby prevent an incident escalating from minor to major. If security responsibility is vague, the chances are that the thing you want done will not happen.

### Do you know what your organisation's main assets are, do you have a list of them, and does this list include information?

If you don't know what you've got, and you don't know what's important, how are you going to direct your security efforts? Also, if you only have a list of your hardware, the chances of you managing the security of your information well are significantly lessened.

### Are specific personnel measures, such as training users or including security in their job descriptions, taken with respect to security?

People commit errors. If they're not trained, they'll do so because they don't know what to do. If they don't realise that they have security responsibilities, the chances are that they'll fail to meet them.

### Do you take steps to prevent unauthorised access to your premises?

Do you know who is on your site at any given time? If you don't, you increase the risk to your business. You could also be in trouble with the fire regulators

### Have you implemented operational controls and procedures to safeguard your information, eg. use of backups, anti virus software, firewalls?

You can't blame people all the time. If you haven't developed an appropriate security infrastructure using appropriate tools, you're asking for trouble.

### Do you control access to information through the effective use of user IDs and passwords?

The humble password is far from dead. Most modern systems provide access control, and can be customised to make access control procedures very flexible; both to manage and use. Also, make sure your people know the rules, especially regarding the sharing of passwords. Have steps been taken to ensure that security requirements are defined and incorporated during system development or met by packaged software solutions? It costs about 10 times more to retrofit controls than to install them at the time of development or implementation.

### Do you have any business continuity plans?

If you don't, you are asking for trouble. You should at least have backups of your important information (see chapter 7). If there's one thing you should do, take a backup, keep it safe (and away from the original) and take another at an appropriate interval.

### Do you ensure that you meet all your legal requirements/obligations, eg licensing, copyright, data protection?

Know the law, make sure you don't foul up your obligations, and always have enough licences for your software.

There's no substitute for expertise, and if you find yourself exposed in such a significant manner, it's probably worth seeking expert advice if you can't address the issues yourself. You can use the above questions periodically, and keep 'score' each time you use them to determine how you're doing. Such an approach can give a degree of internal assurance but, remember, it will not cut too much ice with external auditors (among others).

BS 7799 is a balanced standard, and meeting all its sections will provide a balanced control set. Failure to meet one or more of the questions could easily undermine good preparation against other types of risk.

This is not a one-off exercise, and the process of checking your status against a reasonable benchmark should form a central plank to your information security strategy.

Source: Insight Consulting